Docker & Kuber... Fundamentals

First step into the world of containers and cloud native

Dedicated to my wife kamini.

Author information

For any help please contact :
Amazon Author Page :
amazon.com/author/ajaykumar
Email : ajaycucek@gmail.com ,
 ajaxreso@gmail.com
Linkedin :
https://www.linkedin.com/in/ajaycucek
Facebook :
https://www.facebook.com/ajaycucek
Youtube :
 https://www.youtube.com/channel/UC1uXE
ebtqCLYxVdzirKZGIA
Twitter : https://twitter.com/ajaycucek
Instagram :
https://www.instagram.com/ajaycucek/
Skype : ajaycucek

Table of contents

Book Overview

Book Overview

Docker and Kubernetes. Everyone's talking about them, tons of people are using them, and it is high time we all got our heads around them. And that's the aim of this course, to get you up and running with the most important bits of what are probably the two most important technologies since the cloud itself. It's a no-previous-experience-required course. In fact, it's designed to be your first step into the world of containers and cloud native. So, from the start, we'll cover all the basics of containers. Obviously, we'll be all over Docker and Kubernetes, but we'll also explain microservices and cloud native. Then, as well as the tech, we'll be looking at ways to prepare ourselves and our businesses to thrive in a container world, and we'll discuss the current state of the union. So like, is this stuff ready for your company and your business-critical production environment? Now then, this course is important because Docker and Kubernetes are literally changing the IT world, and if you're involved in IT, which I assume you are, and you want to position yourself as best you can for the future, then you absolutely need to know this stuff. It's just not an option. But you know what? As well as being important, the technologies are a bit special as well. I mean, it's not often a couple of technologies come along and reshape our world like these are. So, two promises from me: One, by the time you're done with the course, you'll be well up to speed, and two, the course is going to be a lot of fun.

Module 1 : Book Introduction

Book Intro

Containers and Kubernetes, they're pretty much front and center on most people's agendas, and rightly so. I mean, we are way beyond the hype phase now. Most people that I speak to, well, they're either deploying it or they're looking at kicking the tires. And if they're not, they are having some serious conversations about it. And I think as well, we've already gone through those treacherous early days where just installing something like Kubernetes was like building a space rocket. So, we're past all of that, and it's actually a really good time to be getting into this stuff. Anyway, look, the ultimate aim of the course is to bring anyone and everyone up to speed with containers in Kubernetes. So that means you can be a developer, a sysadmin, an architect, a manager, whatever, right? This course will get you on track, but what do I mean by on track? Well the title is a bit of a giveaway, Fundamentals, so I'm thinking right at the very least enough to point you in the right direction. Because I get it. The container world's a big place, and it has got more than enough buzzwords and even more projects and companies that are vying for your attention, so we'll help you with that. But as well, I also want you to be able to hold your own when the topic comes up in conversation because believe me, and I've been there myself, you know, when the conversation switches to some shiny new technology, and you've heard about it, but you really don't know it, and of course, I mean, there's no way you're going to admit that, well, the course will help out there because once we're done, you'll be holding your own in container conversations. And it doesn't matter where they are, whether they're coffee machine, in the pub, or even in the boardroom. You definitely won't be embarrassing yourself.

- Agenda

    - Containers Primer
    - Docker
    - Kubernetes
    - Thriving in a Container World
    - Suitable Workloads
    - Enterprise & Production Readiness
    - A Word on Orchestration
    - What Next

Alright, well this is the agenda: What are containers? And this is the very basics, so, like, what is a container like compared to a virtual machine? But as well, I think we'll address the wider picture of microservices and cloud native. Then we'll get into some specifics. First up, we'll do Docker, then we'll do Kubernetes. Then, we'll look at how we can prepare. Now, I mean us as individuals, like how do we prepare, you and me, but we'll also look at how we prepare our teams and our organizations because like it or not, winter is coming, only it's not winter, it's more like spring because this stuff's game changing, and it is great. Either way though, preparation is king. Anyway, after that, we'll talk about some different types of workloads and apps here, and we'll see whether they're good fits for containers. Then, we'll look at how it all fits in with big enterprises. So, we'll be talking a bit around some of the products and companies that offer this stuff as "enterprise grade, " but we'll also look at a few pointers around how some of the large enterprises have onboarded containers in Kubernetes, like what's worked for them and what hasn't. Then we'll talk a bit about orchestration, and we'll wrap it all up with a few pointers on where to go next. And yeah, that's the plan. And when we're all done, like we just said, you will be well and truly prepared to hold your own. Magic! Well, let's get on to our first topic: What actually is a container?

Module 2 : Containers: Primer

Containers: Primer

A proper understanding of containers is fundamental to any journey with Docker and Kubernetes. So, that's what we'll do now, give you an understanding of what a container is. In fact, we'll even see one in action at the end, but as well, we'll talk a bit around what microservices are and what all this cloud-native stuff means.
Module Outline

- The Bad Old Days
- VMware and Hypervisors
- Containers
- Container Demo
- Recap

So, here's the plan: We'll start out by covering a bit of IT history, we'll spend some time talking about virtual machines, pros and cons, then we'll get into containers. We'll see one in action, and then we'll recap the major points. Okay, the bad old days.

The Bad Old Days

Right then, a quick tour of IT history. But you know what? Really important to set the scene and help us understand the why behind containers. Alright, so fundamental to IT and something that I'd hope everyone in IT understands, applications run businesses. No matter what sector you're in these days, banking, retail, airlines, air traffic control, whatever it is your business does, applications are at the center of it. In fact, it's becoming nigh on impossible to distinguish between the business and the applications that power it. They really are one in the same. And you know what? If I've heard it once, I've heard it a million times, no applications, no business, and it gets truer every day. Well, applications run, for the most part, on servers. And back in the day, I'd say definitely early to mid 2000s, most of the time we were doing one app per server. And by servers, I mean big, expensive, physical tin. So yeah, one of these for every app. And the model worked a bit like this: Hey, the business needs a new application for whatever reason, maybe a new product launch or something. Whatever though, the business needs a new app. Well, that means IT needs to go out and buy a new server. That comes with an upfront CapEx cost, but don't forget, it's also got a bunch of OpEx costs. I mean, power and cooling isn't free, and neither is hiring people to build and administer stuff. Okay, but you know what?

Want kind of server does this new application require? How big does it have to be and how fast? And I can tell you from sorry experience, the answers to questions like these were almost always nobody knows. Seriously! Nobody ever knew how big or fast a server had to be. So, IT did the only reasonably thing. They erred on the side of caution, and they went big and fast. And rightly so, right? I mean, the last thing anyone wanted, including the business, was poor performance. I mean, imagine it, unable to carry out business and potentially losing customers and revenue all because IT cheeked out on a server that wasn't fast enough. No, not happening on my shift. So IT bought big and fast, and yeah, you probably know, 99 times out of 100 we ended up with a bunch of massively overpowered servers running at like 5% or 10% of what they were actually capable of. A proper shameful waste of company capital and resources. So, that was the bad old days.

Hello VMware

Then along came VMware, and oh my goodness did the world change for the better! Almost overnight we had this technology that let us take those same over-specced physical servers and squeeze so much more out of them. Literally, a load more bang for the company's buck. So, I guess, well done IT operation's guys. I never doubted for one second that you always knew that those overpowered servers would one day become useful. Well, anyway, keeping on track. Instead of dedicating one physical server to one lonely app, suddenly we could safely and securely run tons of apps on a single physical server. Cue hallelujah music! Seriously, think about it. That scenario of the business coming and saying, hey, we're growing, expanding, diversifying, whatever, and we need a new application, well it's no longer an automatic purchase of an expensive new server. Now we can say, yeah, no sweat. We've already got these servers over here that are barely doing anything. We'll just put the app on one of them. And like I say, almost overnight, though let's not forget, I mean, VMware is a company, and hypervisor technology in general is way more than a decade old now. So, it's not really overnight. It did take time. But here we are in a day and age where 999 times out of 1, 000 we only buy a new server when we genuinely need one. We are properly squeezing stuff onto our servers and sweating those company assets. And like I said, what a better place the IT world is for it. But, and why is there always a but? It's not a perfect solution. Of course it's not.

VM Warts

So, as good as the VMware and the hypervisor model is, it's got a few shortcomings.

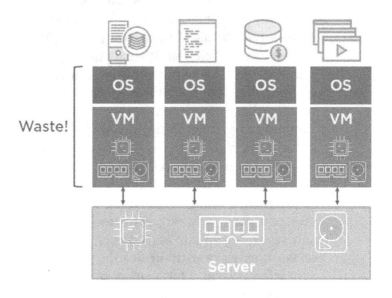

We take a single physical server, and I'm going with a slightly more detailed diagram this time, but we're still high level. So, this is our server. It's got processes, memory, and disk space, and we know we can run a bunch of apps on it. Now, I'm only showing four here to keep the diagram simple. Anyway, to run these four apps, we create four virtual machines, and each one of these is essentially a slice of the physical server's hardware. So let's call this here virtual server 1, and we might've allocated it, I don't know, 25% of the underlying server's processing power. Remember, we're just big picture here. So maybe 25% of CPU, 25% of memory, and 25% of the physical server's disk space. And then, you know what, let's just say we did the same for the rest. Well these are all slices of the real resources in the physical server below. Then, each one of these virtual machines needs its very own dedicated operating system. So, that's four installations of usually Windows or Linux, each of which steals a fair chunk of those resources, CPU, memory, and disk, and it steals them just in order to run. We've not got any applications running yet. This is just the operating system stealing those resources. But that's not all. You may even need four operating system licenses. So right there we've got potential cost already in resources and budget that, I don't know, it just feels like is a waste. I mean, look, as cool as operating systems are, they're a necessary evil. If we could safely and securely run our apps directly on the server hardware without needing an operating system, I tell you what, we definitely would. But back on track. It's not just any potential cost of licensing the operating systems. Each and every one needs feeding and caring for, so admin stuff like security patching, updating, maybe anti-virus management. There's like this whole realm of operational baggage that comes with each one. And VMware and other hypervisors, as great as they absolutely are, they don't do much to help us with this. So, yeah, VMware and the hypervisor model, it changed the world into a much better place, but there's still issues, and there's still gains to be made, which leads us nicely onto containers.

Containers

Alright, that's definitely more than enough setting the scene. Let's finally explain what a container is, and you know what, let's have a picture to help.

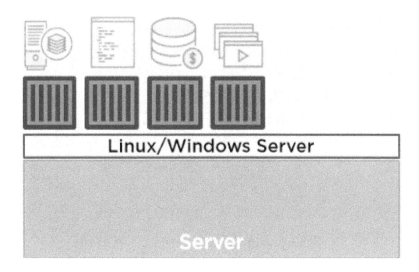

Okay, so to keep it simple, we start out with the same physical server. You know what? Let's go with the same four business apps just to keep things fair. Well, instead of installing a hypervisor down here and then four virtual machines and operating systems on top, each with its own baggage and overhead remember, well instead of all that, we install one operating system, just one. Then, on top of that, we create four containers. Now we'll come to it in a minute, but each of these containers is a slice of the operating system. Well, it's inside these

13

containers that we run our apps, one-to-one
again, one app per container. Now, we're
being a bit high level here, but you know
what? I am purposefully drawing the
containers smaller than I drew the virtual
machines because they actually are smaller,
and they're more efficient. Though, aside
from that, the model kind of looks similar,
right? In fact, let's see a side-by-side
comparison.

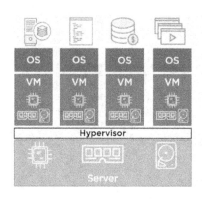 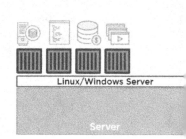

See how on the left here on top of the
hypervisor we create a virtual machine?
Well all that is is a software construct
dressed up to look and feel exactly like a
physical server. So like we said before, each
one's got its own virtual CPUs, virtual RAM,
virtual disks, virtual network cards, the
whole shebang. Then on top of that, we said
we'd install an operating system, and to each
one of those operating systems, the virtual
machine below it looks exactly like a physical
server. It doesn't know the difference.
Anyway, look, we already said that these
operating systems have CapEx and OpEx
costs. I mean, there's patching, upgrading,
driver support, all that stuff. But look here.

14

Each operating system also consumes resources from the physical server, effectively stealing resources. So each and every operating system steals CPU. It steals memory, and it steals disk space. Well you know what? We could call this model the hungry operating system model. Each and every one is eating into everything, admin time, system resources, budgets, you name it. Oh, and you know what? Gets worse. Each one is a potential attack vector. So seriously, somebody remind me why we have them. Anyway, look, back to the container model here. It's only got one operating system. So, take a physical server, install an operating system, and then we essentially carve, or slice, that operating system into secure containers. Then, inside the containers we run an app. Net result: We get rid of pretty much all this fat here. It's just gone, meaning we've got all of this free space over here to spin up more containers and more apps for the business. Love it! Oh, and you know what? These apps in the containers here, they start like, I don't know, just so fast. It's ideal for situations where you're spinning things up and tearing things down on demand because there's no virtual machine and no extra operating system to boot before your app can start. No, in the container model, the OS is down here, and it's already running. So all of these apps up here in the container model are securely sharing a single operating system down here. Net net, most containerized apps spin up in probably less than a second, and you've only got one operating system that's stealing resources and demanding admin time. So that's it. Tell you what, let's see one in action.

Container Demo

Okay, quick demo time, and you know what? Don't be put off by the site of the command line in a big picture course. It's going to be a really simple demo. And you know what? Everything that we do here can be done either through a GUI, or even better, automated through APIs and orchestration tools. Anyway, I've got a machine here running Docker. Now, it doesn't matter where or what that machine is. So it could be a virtual machine in the cloud or a bare-metal server in your datacenter or even your laptop running Docker Desktop. It really doesn't matter. Docker is Docker. It runs on VMs, bare metal, your laptop, whatever. In fact, do you know what? Let's drop our picture in up here.

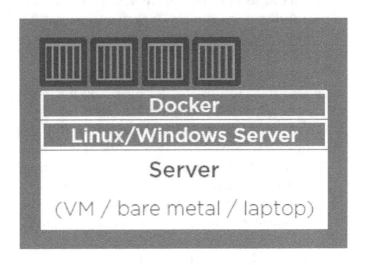

So I'm logged on to the host here, and it's got Docker installed. Now Docker does Linux and Windows, and generally speaking, at the kind of high level we're at at least,

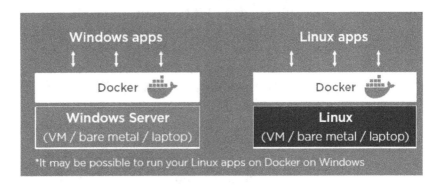

Docker on Linux will only run Linux apps, and Docker on Windows only runs Windows apps. Now, look, there are ways to get Linux apps running on Docker on Windows, fair enough, but for us right now, at the kind of level we're at, it's really best to think of

Linux apps running on Docker on Linux and
Windows apps run on Docker on Windows.
In ubuntu docker host :
docker image ls
Anyway, look, I've downloaded a single
image here to this Docker host, and it's
called ctr-demo. Now, you can think of an
image as a prepacked application, or if
you're a techie guy, maybe think of it as like
a VM template. Basically, it's got everything
wrapped up into a single bundle that you
need to run an application. This one happens
to contain a web server that runs some static
content.
ubuntu@Docker-host:-$ docker container
run -d --name web -p 8000:8080
ajaycucek/docker-demo:2
So, to fire up a container from this image,
we'll use this long command, which in case
you're interested says run me a new
container, base it off of the image that I just
downloaded, call it this name, and then
expose it on this network port. Yeah, there's
other options in there, but for us right now,
this is all we need to know. And check that
out. This number is the unique ID of the
container, and it tells us that it's already up
and running. So, I don't know how fast that
was, but less than a second probably.
Now, there's commands and the likes to get
details of running containers, obviously, but
all that we need to know is the IP address of
our server here, that's this number up here,
and that we exposed it on port 8080.

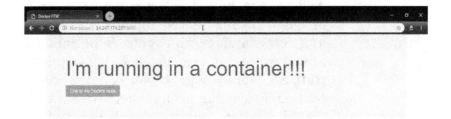

So, if we switch to a new browser tab here and put in that IP and port, boom, there is our web server. So, let me recap just in case something wasn't clear. I downloaded an image. Think of that as a prepacked application. In our case, it included a web server, some content for the web server to display, and an embedded command that would automatically start that web server when we spin the image up as a container. Well, once that image was downloaded, and you download these from container registries like Docker Hub, which for want of a better analogy is a bit like the App Store, but just for containerized apps. Anyway, once we've got the image, we told Docker to fire it up as a container. We gave it a name, and we exposed it on a network port. And you know what? Docker just made it happen, and fast. Then, obviously, we verified it with a browser. Good stuff. But you know what? Because containers are a lot like virtual machines, just faster and more lightweight, ubuntu@Docker-host:-$ docker stop web well, we can stop them like this, and if we go back to the web page and hit refresh, we see, as expected, it's not running anymore. But back here to start it again, and refresh the browser again, and we're back in business. And no joke, how simple was that? Get an image with your desired app in it, fire it up as a new container, and you're in business. Stop it, restart it, even delete it. It's simple stuff. So, there you go. If you've never seen a container in action before, you have now, though don't be underwhelmed. This stuff really comes into its own at scale. Anyway, look, let's wrap up the module by mentioning microservices architecture and a bit on cloud native, and of course, we'll be recapping the major points that we've already covered.

Recap

So, apps run businesses. No apps, no business, all that jazz, and in the old days, we spent way too much of pretty much everything getting those apps up and running. It took too long, it cost too much, and it resulted in a buttload of waste. Well, along came VMware and friends, and all of the sudden things got better. Lead times collapsed, costs came down, and utilization, I mean, through the roof we were cooking on gas. Only progress waits for no one, and while we were rocking it with VMware, the Linux world was plowing away developing the technologies required to run containers, which are faster, cheaper, and give us even better utilization. Now, we can use containers like virtual machines. I mean, for a while now Docker, Inc. has been running a program called modernizing traditional apps where you effectively lift and shift old legacy apps into containers. And that's all good, it works, and it's a step in the right direction, but containers offer so much more, and this is where terms like microservices and cloud native start getting thrown around. So, winding the clock back a bit again. Legacy apps, or monolithic apps as we sometimes call them, these are those monstrous apps where everything that the app does is pretty much baked into a single binary, which is just a fancy name for a computer program. So everything lumped into a single program. Maybe your app has a web front end, a shopping cart, inventory manager, search, authentication, I don't know, a checkout service, you name it. In the monolithic design, all of that functionality gets baked into a single program, and without getting into detail, it's just a nightmare from a developer perspective. If you want to update or fix, let's say, just the search part of the app, it is a whole big exercise on the entire code base. So, you're hacking the entire app, and you're testing, and you're recompiling the whole thing. Not a lot of fun, and you know what, more than a bit risky. And on the operations front, if you've got an issue, let's just say with the same search functionality again, the only way to roll out a fix, because everything's lumped into a single program remember, so the only way to roll out a fix is to take the entire app down. Good luck getting the business to agree to that. Fortunately, cloud native and microservices on the other hand, these break out all of those different components and make each one its own little mini app or mini service. I mean, they all still talk to each other to make the full app experience, but updating that search feature, all of the sudden, that just became way easier for the developer and the operator. So now the developer only needs to touch the search code when it updates the search feature, and ops, they only need to roll out the new version of the search service. No more taking the entire beast down just to update one part. And you know what? That's the essence of microservices and cloud native, build, deploy, and manage apps in a way that lends itself to modern business requirements, or cloud computing requirements as we often call them. So, no, it isn't really anything to do with deploying on the cloud. I mean, you can absolutely run a cloud-native app in your on-prem datacenter. You see, cloud native is all about how the app's built and managed, so we can do things like scale the front end independent of the back end. And like we said, you can iterate on each feature independently. Now, we could talk about this all day, but time is of the essence, so let me finish with this: In a way, containers are virtualization 2.0. They improve on nearly everything offered by hypervisors, and they pave the way for more modern cloud native and microservices applications. Though, do you know what? Don't expect them to replace VMs, I mean, not entirely because, well, I mean, in a lot of cases, they'll live side by side. I mean, sure, plenty of people are container only, especially startups and those people that are 100% in the public cloud, but in most enterprises, and a lot of other places, we'll be seeing containers and VMs sitting side by side, and you know what, even the occasional mainframe lurking around in the background. Okay, what have we got next? Next on the agenda is a closer look at Docker, the company and the technology. See you there.

Module 3 : Docker

Docker

Docker, Docker, Docker. No conversation about containers or even microservices is complete without Docker, which I think is, without question, the company and the technology that gave us modern containers. So cheers! Nice one Docker. So, this is how we'll do this. Docker is, at the very least, two things: There's the company Docker, Inc., and there's the technology Docker. And as we'll see, they're closely linked, but they are not the same. So, we'll talk about them separately, and we'll start with the company. And you know what? We might even do a bit of a demo. We'll see. Let's go talk about Docker the company.

Docker, Inc.

So, Docker, Inc., big D Docker or capital D Docker. It's a technology startup from San

Francisco, and it's the main sponsor behind the open-source container technology with the same name. But you know what? It is way more than just that, but let's start at the beginning. Docker the company didn't actually start out life as Docker, nor was it really anything to do with changing the way that we build, ship, and run our applications. Originally, it was a company called dotCloud that provided a developer platform on top of Amazon Web Services. So, you know, like taking AWS and then layering this kind of uniform developer experience on top. Only that wasn't working so much as a business, and at around about 2013 they really needed something different. And it just so happens in one of those twists of fate they'd been using containers to build their platform on top of AWS, and, and this is the important bit, they had this home-grown tech that they built as an internal tool to help them spin up and manage their containers. And cutting a long story short, and I wasn't there myself, but this is the gist, they needed something new. They looked at this in-house tech for building containers and thought what if we give this to the world and build a business around it? Well obviously, that in-house tech was Docker, and here we are today where Docker has literally changed the technology world in a similar way to VMware, though arguably, Docker's changed things in a deeper and a more fundamental way. Anyway, the name Docker actually comes from a British colloquialism that's a conjunction of dock and worker. So somebody who works at a dock, or a shipping port, you put the two together, get rid of the work, and you get Docker. And I really like it. It's short and catchy. Anyway, like we said, around 2013 the company called dotCloud made a humongous pivot, and it changed its business from being this company that provided a developer platform on top of AWS to a company that changed the way we build, ship, and run software. Look, it gave us the gift of containers. Sounds cheesy I know, but it's true. Well, since then, as a company, they have taken in trailer loads of venture cash, I think raising something like $200, 000, 000 in just a couple of years and even more since. But you know what? In those early days, it felt like yeah they were hard at work building the technology, but not with such a great vision on how to make it into a viable business. Now, of course, this is my opinion from the outside with, okay, a bit of internal access. And you know what? I mean no disrespect to anyone involved with Docker, quite the opposite actually. I've nothing but respect for what they've built. But yeah, back in the early days, it really felt like it was lacking in a business plan. Anyway, look, that was then, and this is now, and these days, I reckon they've got a solid business plan. In fact, now, one of the main focuses of Docker, Inc. is selling an enterprise-grade container management platform and providing world-class support. Well, look, I think without getting into too much detail, that's Docker, Inc., a tech startup from the Bay Area. They gave the world the gift of Docker and easy-to-use containers, and these days they're in the business of orchestrating and supporting containerized apps at scale with a focus on enterprises. Magic! Now let's turn our attention to the technology.

Docker the Technology

Okay, let me try and give you Docker, the technology, in like one or two sentences. Containers are like fast lightweight virtual machines, and Docker makes running our apps inside of containers really easy. Now, we're going to dig a bit deeper, but that really is the main takeaway. Docker makes running apps inside of containers really easy. Anyway, the Docker application, if you will, is open source, and like more open-source software these days, it lives on GitHub. And let me say I appreciate that in the past a lot of people, and I want to say especially enterprises, but maybe that's just because I spent most of my career in large enterprises, anyway, there was definitely a stigma around open-source software in the past. And I'm not bothered about getting into the politics of that other than to say those days, thank goodness, are well and truly behind us now. In fact, open-source software is eating the world.
Community Edition (CE)

- Open source
- Lots of contributors
- Quick release cycle

Enterprise Edition (EE)

- Slower release cycle
- Additional features
- Official support

Well, the open-source Docker technology, generally called the Community Edition, or CE, it's free to use, and you can contribute back, and please do. You'll be in good company because the list of people and companies that have contributed, wow, it's like the who's who of the technology world. There's your Red Hatters, IBMers, and I know IBM owns Red Hat, but there's Microsoft, you name it. All the big players are contributors. Plus, most of them are supporting it as well. Now then, as well as the Community Edition, Docker, Inc., the company, sells and supports an Enterprise Edition, which is essentially the same technology stack, only it's on a slower release cadence, I guess to keep it more stable, but it gets a few extra features and obviously an enterprise-class support contract. Either way though, Community Edition and Enterprise Edition are both about running and managing apps inside of containers. In fact, we call apps running in containers containerized apps. Now, you know what? I think we will do a demo. I was going to go through the workflow now, so let's do a quick demo, and I'll just explain the workflow as we go. It'll be better this way anyway.

Docker Demo

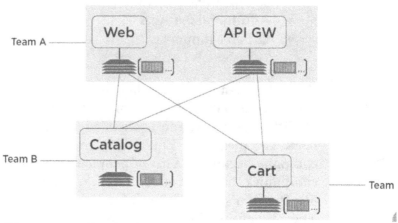

Okay, so earlier in the course we touched a bit on microservices. I think maybe we said something like modern cloud-native apps are built from lots of small parts that work together to form a useful app. So, maybe you've got an app with a web front-end service, an API gateway, a catalog, shopping cart, whatever. Well, in the cloud-native microservices world, each one of these services gets coded separately, and each one lives in its own container. And you know what? You can even have different teams responsible for each one. Now importantly, what this means is that each one of those services can be fixed, updated, whatever, independent of the rest. But of course, they all talk to each other to form that useful app.

```
var express = require('express'),
    app = express();

app.set('views', 'views');
app.set('view engine', 'pug');

app.get('/', function(req, res) {
    res.render('home', {
  });
});

app.listen(8080);
module.exports.getApp = app;
```

**Well, this is some super simple code that
runs a web server. If you're a developer, you
see stuff like this every day, but if you're not
a developer, all it is is some application
source code, and when we run it, it's going to
display a web page. Alright, so what we'll do
is we'll briefly walk through how to get this
code up and running as a container, with the
emphasis on brief. We've got some code, and
this is the workflow we'll follow.**

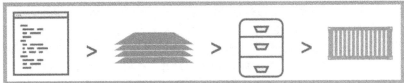

**We'll take the code and build it into a
Docker image. Now, an image is like a
stopped container or maybe a template for
how to build a container. Anyway, we'll
build an image. Then we'll push that to a
registry. After that, we'll start a container
from it. Dead easy.
In window command prompt :**

C:\docker-demo> docker image build -t ajaycucek/docker-demo:2

Step one then, containerize this app. Now I'm on a machine with Docker installed, it's actually my Windows laptop, and all of my code and dependencies are right here in this folder and any folders beneath it. So I just go docker image build, this is telling Docker to build me an image, and we'll call it this, and then saying period here says build the image out of all of the files in this directory and below. And that's away building. Now, while it does it, all Docker's doing here is taking our source code and doing all the hard work to package it as a container, or as an image actually, because remember, an image is like a stopped container. Anyway, let me bend space time here a bit until this is done.

In window command prompt :

C:\docker-demo> docker image ls ajaycucek/docker-demo:2

Okay, we should have a shiny new image here. Right, but you know what? It's our source code all packaged and ready to use as a container.

C:\docker-demo> docker image push ajaycucek/docker-demo:2

Now, the next step, and I mean after testing and everything, but normally we'd push this image to a registry. I'm just going to push it to Docker Hub, but you can have your own on-prem or private registries. The workflow is the same. Okay, a bit more tinkering with space time, and here it is on Docker Hub.

Go to your url in browser like this :

https://cloud.docker.com/repository/registry-1.docker.io/ajaycucek/docker-demo

Marvelous! So, application containerized and now pushed to a registry.
C:\docker-demo> docker container run -d -- name web -p 8000:8080 ajaycucek/docker-demo:2
That just leaves us with the last step to run it, which we saw from a previous lesson. Run me a container, give it a name, make it available on the network, and base it on this image here we just built. And it's like greased lightning.

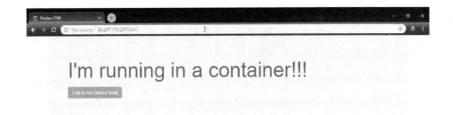

So if we open a browser tab, this is our local machine here where the container's running, I think it was port 8000, and is if by magic. Thing of beauty. Alright, well let's recap what we've learned in this module.

Docker Summary

Okay, we said Docker is at least two things. There's one, the company, and there's two, the tech, and yeah, they're related. We said the company Docker is out of San Francisco, and they are all about helping people move to containers and providing an enterprise-class platform with the usual type of support agreements that most enterprises demand. Then there's the technology. This is all about running your business applications inside of containers. And I think like we saw in the demo, you just take your application code and you build it into an image, then you store that in a registry somewhere, on-prem, in the cloud, it's your call, and you use that image to spin up your app as containers. And that's it. It's not rocket science, and that's actually the beauty of it, it's simple. But, as simple as it is, it is absolutely key to moving to a modern cloud-native microservices design, which I know is a bunch of buzzwords, but it's all vital if you want your business and your applications to be able to roll with the demands of the modern world. Okay, well, it's all well and good running a single container on your laptop like we've just shown you. It's a whole different world though doing it at scale. And you know what? Scale is where the real world is. So, to help us with this, there's two things I'll mention here. I mean, there's other options as well, but for us in this course, there's Docker Swarm and there's Kubernetes. but for us now on this course, we're going to focus on Kubernetes because to be honest, it's where most of the action is. So, see you there.

Module 4 : Kubernetes

Kubernetes

Kubernetes. Everyone's talking about it, and
to be fair, loads of people are using it. So,
this is what we'll cover: We'll set the scene
with a bit of history and background stuff,
the kind of stuff you really need to know
before taking your first steps. Then, we'll
just go for it. What is it? How does it work?
And what does it do for us? Then we'll finish
with a recap. So, let's do it.

Kubernetes: History

Okay, way back like once upon a time ago,
Google was taking over the internet. Google
began to dominate the internet, more and
more of the tech that was powering it was
actually running in containers. So, things
like search, but also Gmail and a bunch of
the other stuff, behind the scenes, it was all
running on containers. Now, remember, this
is way back when, like long before Docker
and all the cool stuff we've got today. So,
Google was running search and stuff on
containers, and obviously search, and even
Gmail and the likes, they're pretty

humongous. I mean, we're talking like billions of containers a day stuff here, which would be right, seeing as every good search runs in its own container. Well, at scale like that, you just can't have humans pushing buttons, so what they did was they built a couple of in-house systems to help. First, they built something called Borg, quality name, then they built Omega. So, Borg came first, and as you do, you learned a bunch of stuff, and they fed that into Omega. Then, for whatever reasons, they decided to build another system, obviously learning from both Borg and Omega, and they made this new one open source, and lo, Kubernetes was born. So, Kubernetes came out of Google, and it's open source. And these days, it's the superstar project for the Cloud Native Computing Foundation, and to say it's gone from strength to strength, wow, that would be an epic understatement. I mean, today, as I'm presenting this, well, I mean, where do I start? From a back-end perspective, it is backed by pretty much everyone. I mean, the cloud players are all over it, and so are the traditional IT vendors. So your big three cloud providers, Amazon, Azure, and Google, they all offer hosted Kubernetes services, and so does IBM and a bunch of the others. But it doesn't stop there. You can get Kubernetes for on-prem, and you know what? Most of them can be backed by enterprise-class support contracts. So everyone's behind it, meaning they're contributing to its development and they're providing support contracts. As well though, on the technology or the feature front, seriously, it is one of the most extensive platforms I've known. In fact, it's probably the most extensive, like it does stateless, stateful, batch work, long running. It does security, storage, networking, serverless, or functions as a service, machine learning. Honestly, we could be here all day. There is not a lot that Kubernetes can't do. And all of the stuff it can do, it can pretty much to anywhere. Like we said, in the cloud and on-prem in you datacenter, and even on your laptop when you're developing. Well, this is becoming a bit of a love fest, and I don't want that, so just one more thing before we dive in a bit. The name Kubernetes, it's Greek for helmsman or captain, the helmsman being the person who steers the ship, which I guess is why they picked it. I mean, after all, we have got this nautical theme going on in the container ecosystem. Oh yeah, and you'll see it shortened to this quite a lot, the 8 replacing the 8 characters between the K and the S, and some people pronounce this kates. You know what though, that'll do for background. Time to look at what it actually does.

Kubernetes: The Short and Skinny

Scheduling, scaling, healing, updating...

start | stop | delete ...

Okay, what Kubernetes does, and I like the tag line saying, seriously, it does most things. Anyway, if you've been following along, you'll know a bit about Docker, which at its core, Docker provides the mechanics for starting and stopping individual containers, which in the grand scheme of things is pretty low-level stuff. Well, Kubernetes, it doesn't care about lower-level stuff like that. Kubernetes cares about higher-level stuff, like how many containers to run in, maybe which nodes to run them on, and things like knowing when to scale them up or down or even how to update your containers without downtime. Now then, this is cheesy, so give me a chance. If you think about your application as a musical masterpiece, I know, bear with me, if you did that, it'd be made up of lots of different musical notes from

36

different instruments. There'd be violins, maybe they'd be front-end services, and I don't know, maybe the brass section would be the back end or whatever, but when they play together, they form this amazing musical experience. Well, if you've seen an orchestra, you know that there's a conductor at the front, and that person's in charge, and she's doing things like telling the trombones when to come in, how many violins, how loud, all of that stuff. Well, applications are similar. Loads of different parts that need to know how and where to run, which network to operate on, how many instances are required to meet demand, and probably a load more. And if this is the case, which it is, then Kubernetes is the conductor. So it's basically issuing commands to Docker instances, telling them when to start and stop containers and how to run them, sort of. And like with the orchestra, when all of this stuff comes together, they form this amazing application experience. Anyway, that was cheesy, so I hope it was useful. A bit more technical though, I guess if you know VMware at all, maybe think of Docker as ESXi, that low-level hypervisor. Then Kubernetes, I suppose, would be vCenter that sits above a bunch of hypervisors.

K8s Control Plane

Anyway, at the kind of high level we're at, we'd have a Kubernetes cluster down here to host our applications, and it can be anywhere. Well, each of these nodes is running some Kubernetes software and a container runtime. Usually the container runtime is Docker or containerd, but others do exist. The point is there's a container runtime on every node so that every node can run containers. Then sitting above all of this is the brains of Kubernetes, and that's making the decisions, like the conductor in the orchestra.

Desired: 2   1

Actual:

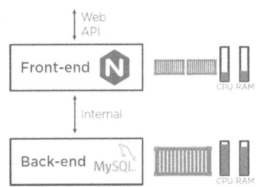

Well, assume we've got a simple app with a web front end and a persistent back end. The web front end is maybe containerized NGINX, and let's say it's containerized MySQL on the back end.

Desired: 2   1

Actual: 2   1

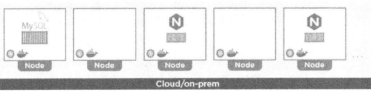

We tell Kubernetes maybe we want a single container on the back end and give it a lot of resources, like CPU and RAM, but on the front end, tell you what, we'll have two

39

containers, but keep these smaller, and
Kubernetes deploys it. So one of the
things Kubernetes does is decides which
nodes to run stuff on, and it'll look
something like this. And that's fine, but

	N	MySQL
Desired:	2	1
Actual:	4	1

let's say load on the front end increases, and
those two containers are not enough. Okay,
no issue. Kubernetes is watching, so it sees
the situation, and maybe it spins up two
more, and it does it without a human getting
involved. So literally, load goes up on the
front end, and Kubernetes has enough
intelligence not just to sit there and suffer.
No, it spins up more containers. Problem
averted. But the same goes if the load
decreases. It's automagic. Kubernetes sees
the drop in load, and it scales back down.
Oh, and it's the same if a node fails or
something. Seriously, Kubernetes is a
fighter. It sees the node go down, and it
doesn't run away and hide, and it doesn't
freeze and hope the situation isn't
happening. No chance. Kubernetes fights. So
remember up here we asked for two web
front ends, but right now we've only got one.

Kubernetes observes this, and it fixes it, and we call that self-healing. Now, look, I appreciate this is really high-level stuff, and I am oversimplifying, but you get it. We tell Kubernetes what we want, and Kubernetes makes it happen. Then when things change, increased load, failed nodes, whatever, Kubernetes deals with it, and who doesn't want that? Anyway, remember, Docker's doing all the low-level container spinney up spinney down stuff, but it only does it when Kubernetes tells it to, meaning in this respect, Kubernetes is managing a bunch of Docker nodes. And look, again, we're ridiculously high level. For now though, I think that's it. Oh, no, one more thing. But you know what? You'll love this.

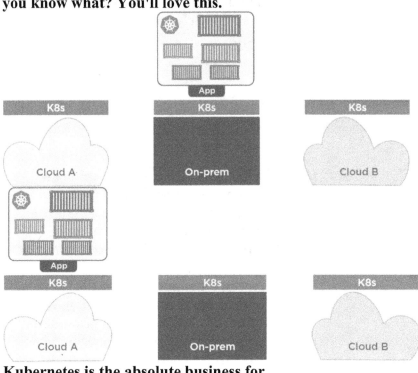

Kubernetes is the absolute business for decoupling your applications from the underlying infrastructure. So, we've said Kubernetes runs everywhere. Kubernetes on-prem, Kubernetes in the cloud, it's all the same, meaning if your apps run on Kubernetes, it is a piece of cake migrating them on and off the cloud or even from one cloud to another. No joke. I mean, unless you're writing your apps to be tightly coupled to the services of one particular cloud, which ideally you wouldn't, but yeah, I understand why we sometimes do, but assuming you're not writing your apps to be locked to a specific cloud, then you can absolutely move seamlessly between one cloud and another and even on and off the cloud, which I think you'll agree has the potential to be huge going forward. Anyway, look, that's definitely enough. Let's do a quick recap.

Recap

Okay, Kubernetes. It's all about managing containerized apps at scale, and the focus is very much on the app. Anyway, it came out of Google where it's got this illustrious ancestral heritage of managing containers at whopping scale. It is open source, and you know what? It's the poster child for the Cloud Native Computing Foundation, which actually, the CNCF is the leading foundation driving the development and adoption of cloud-native technologies. And as you'd probably guess, its members are all of the leading tech companies, large and small.

Now speaking of vendors, they are literally all over Kubernetes, like all the major cloud players have it, and the traditional on-premises vendors, they love it as well. I think the take-home point, Kubernetes is everywhere, and everyone is offering it, and for the most part, you can get it with solid support contracts. Good stuff.

On the more technical side though, we build a Kubernetes cluster to host our applications, and it can be anywhere, on-premises in your own datacenter or just about any cloud, and even your laptop when you're developing. Well, once we've got that, we package our apps, tell Kubernetes what they should look like, and then we just sit back, and we let Kubernetes do all the hard stuff of deploying and managing. So things like scaling, self-healing, running updates, all that stuff, no sweat. Kubernetes does it. I mean, there's obviously some up-front work from us to do like the packaging and set some of the thresholds and the likes, but honestly, with actually not a huge amount of effort from us, Kubernetes really can manage our apps, which definitely is magic, but capping it all off is the fact that it decouples our apps from any underlying environment, meaning we can switch between clouds, we can move back on-prem, and even back to the cloud again. It's all pretty easy with Kubernetes. Any you know what? In my opinion, it's got the brightest future of any technology I can remember. And on that note, that's it. I mean, there's a ton more in our Getting Started with Kubernetes course, but for us here and now, we're switching tack, and we're going to look at how we can prepare for all of this.

Module 5 : Preparing to Thrive in a Container World

Preparing to Thrive in a Container World

Okay, so we're at the point where most people have heard of containers, and actually, quite a few have gotten awareness of the potential changes they bring, and sometimes they're worried, which, actually, I think is fair enough. I mean, change represents the unknown, and a lot of us, including a lot of organizations, just don't like unknowns, or, at least, they're wary of them. That all said though, more often than not, people accept that at some point they're going to have to deal with containers, which is why I'm always asked, how can we prepare? Well, obviously, that's the topic for this module.

Agenda :

- Individual preparation
- Organizational preparation

How can we prepare ourselves and our organizations so that we can not only live, but thrive in a world of containers? And we'll look at it from these two aspects: One, how do we prepare ourselves as individuals, you know, make sure we look after our own careers and make sure we're personally ready for the opportunities that are coming, but also, we'll talk about how we can prepare our teams and organizations. So, exciting times ahead, and everybody has their chance to be a winner or a loser. It's up to you. Let's crack on.

Individual Preparedness

Alright then, protecting our own backs. Hey, we've all got to do it. Anyway, on the personal-preparedness front, the two things you need to survive and thrive are knowledge and experience. Now, I know that no two of you watching this course are the same. I mean, some of you are going to be hands on, like developers, sys admins, dev ops. Some of you are going to be architects, some management. We've probably got the full set. Well, if you're one of the hands-on type, just keep doing what you do best and get your hands on this stuff, but get them filthy. Seriously, it's never been easier to play around with new tech. I mean, in the Docker and Kubernetes space, you can play around on your laptop. I reckon everyday I'm using Docker Desktop, which if you don't know is free software from Docker, Inc., and it runs on Windows and Mac, and what you get is a development Docker and Kubernetes environment. In fact, you know what? Some of the demos from earlier in the course were done on my laptop. Magic. But you can also run this stuff in the cloud, so like on your own cloud instances or one of the many prepackaged hosted services. I think, for example, in the Kubernetes space, you can build your own clusters on vanilla cloud instances, or you can use one of the hosted services like EKS from Amazon Web Services or AKS from Azure or even GKE from Google, which is my personal favorite. As well as that though, there's free online playgrounds like Play with Docker and Play with Kubernetes. The point is there are no excuses for not getting your hands filthy with dirt. Again, the point is get learning, and get your hand dirty. Now then, if you're not a hands-on person, or maybe you're not in a hands-on role, no worries. Crack on with this course. Its whole raison d'etre is to clue you up on the basics so that at the very least you know what you're talking about next time you get asked. And I promise, by the end, any fears or doubts you might have before, you'll be like, what was that all about? You will be more than ready to get contacting your peers and talking and planning.

Organization Preparedness

Okay, the million crypto coin question. How can we prepare our teams and organizations for containers? And this one is a bit trickier, but it's still very doable. Well, first and foremost is acceptance. Your teams and organizations have to accept that containers are coming. And even if you don't think they're coming to your organization, I don't know, you might be surprised. And that's not me thinking that I know more about your business than you do. I'm just saying there's a change you might be surprised. Let me give you an example. A while back, like when cloud computing was finding its feet, the owner of a large database and technology company was on the record as saying the cloud was this made-up thing and would have zero impact on his mega business. This is a true story by the way. Well, unfortunately for him and his business, people like Amazon and Microsoft took it a bit more seriously, and in many ways, they saw what was coming, and they adapted themselves to thrive. Well, fast-forward to today where AWS and Microsoft Azure are tearing things up, well, guess what? This megacorp that ignored the cloud is watching its competitors eat its lunch while it plays this massive game of cloud catch up. And you know what? Potentially, it's never going to make up the lost ground. Moral of this story, and don't get me wrong here, you know your business way better than I do, just do yourself a favor and take a bit of a step back and have a proper look at how and where containers might be able to improve your business in IT. You might be surprised. Anyway, so the first thing is definitely to acknowledge that those things over there on the horizon are containers, and they're probably heading our way. Next up, ask around. Ascertain, first of all, whether or not you've already got containers in your environment, potentially under the radar. I mean, let's learn from our past with the public cloud. How many of you guys, like me, were operating in blissful ignorance while teams and individuals were procuring services and infrastructure from AWS under the radar. I got burned. Shadow IT. So get out there and determine whether or not you've already got containers. Have you got containers? Sounds like a disease. Anyway, after that, start thinking and talking about good areas to start using them. Now, generally speaking, developers are going to love them, and a great place for developers to start is continuous integration and continuous delivery. But, keep a tag on things because the chances are they'll like them so much they'll start using them anywhere they can, which is good in the long run, it just needs to be done right. So you know what actually, what a lot of companies do, especially the bigger ones, is they set up some kind of SWAT team, and they give them a new project or some area of the business that's a good fit for a testing ground. So like you section off this area of the business or whatever for a specialized team, and you have them get into the whole thing, Docker, Kubernetes, microservices, you name it, the whole shebang, and you get them to learn it, and you get them to deploy it. And once they've done that maybe once or twice, then you get them to become ambassadors or whatever for the wider company. So like a seeding team. Pull it off in a new project or two, then deliver it to the wider organization. And as well as that, while that's going on, messaging and education is massive. Now, developers are great, but it's important not to ignore infrastructure and ops, especially I think with Kubernetes because that's arguably got more on the ops front, like deploying and then also managing your apps. And guess what? For this to work in your production environments, the same old production rules apply. I'm thinking things like you're going to want resilient infrastructure to run these new apps on, you're going to want monitoring, you're going to want logging, you're going to need orchestration, and as always, do not leave it until the last minute. Now, I'm waffling a bit, so let me close out with this. The golden rule here really is just to talk. Get dev and ops talking, get management talking, and then get doing. And like we said, start small, but dream big. I can't believe I just said that, but it's true, right? Do it! It's how just about everybody I deal with is doing it. So recapping, a small specialist team, have them work on something small, but take the holistic view, and then when they've done it successfully, seed it throughout the rest of the business. It's a tried and tested approach. Okay, one last thing. You probably want to start thinking about who pays for this stuff, like whose budget will it come out of, which in turn quite often dictates who owns it. But you know what? That's probably the best advice I can give for how to prepare yourself and your organization.

Recap

So that was an easy module. Get prepared. In recapping though, I think a couple of takeaway points are look, containers are common. In fact, they might already be where you are, and maybe, just maybe, you might not know about them. So do some digging. They're either here already, or they're at the front door. Which leads to the second point. When they arrive, I'm telling you, they spread like crazy. So, prepare yourself individually with the necessary skills, but also prepare your organizations by getting into Docker and Kubernetes, but also the things like logging and monitoring and all the other stuff that you need for a production deployment. Then, make sure all the relevant teams and people are talking, especially developers and operations if that's how your organization's structured. Because you know what? These are exciting times, and I'm probably going to get a bit carried away here, but make no mistake, the winners and the losers are still being decided. Now, on the individual front, there'll be people who carve out stellar careers and build stellar companies, but on the flip side, there'll be people who struggle to keep up, and unfortunately, some who get utterly steamrollered by the whole thing. But like I keep saying, it's still early days, and you know what? This is going to sound horrifically cheesy, but you have absolutely got the power to choose your own destiny here. Literally grab containers by the scruff of their neck, and make them work for your career and your organization. And on the winners and losers front, it's the same for companies and organizations and even IT departments. There'll be some who see this comment and set themselves up to benefit, and there'll be some that batten down the hatches and just hope it blows over. And in most cases, it's not going to blow over. Well, I can't see it at least. But I think as well we said, within organizations, look at maybe setting up specialized teams that dive into the deep end on some safe project or whatever, and then once they're good at it, start getting it out there to the wider organization. Okay, coming up next, we're going to talk about the types of applications that containers are good for and maybe some that they're not so good for.

Module 6 : Suitable Workloads

Suitable Workloads

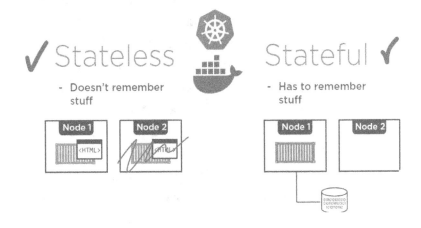

Okay, a question I still get asked about containers is whether or not they can be used for stateful apps, so apps that persist data, or if they're just good for stateless. And you know what, if I'm being honest, in the past, that was one of those, well, I mean, yeah they're obviously amazing at stateless stuff, but they can do stateful as well, only that last bit, I don't know, it always felt a bit like I was trying too hard or even trying to convince myself a bit. But you know what?

That was then, and this is now, and since at least 2018, both Docker and Kubernetes have gotten really good at doing stateful. And you know what? We'll get into the detail in a minute, but for now, maybe we could do with a definition. But, before I get into this, stateless and stateful can mean different things to different people, so I'm throwing this out there as the definition that we'll work with. So I'm saying a stateful app, or a stateful service, is one that absolutely has to remember stuff. Like if a stateful app stops or crashes or the node it's running on dies, well it abso-freakin-lutely has to come back up without forgetting anything, and a database is the usual example. So when you first fire up a database, it probably looks something like this. So the database app is running in a container here on node 2, and it's using a volume to actually store the data. That's our state. And when it's very first created, it's empty, but as things crack on, it starts storing data. Then, if things go pop, for whatever reason, it doesn't matter, but what does matter is that restarting the service may be over here, it absolutely has to come back up with all the data that was previously stored. If you started here fresh again with no data, well what's the point? So for us, that's stateful. It has to remember stuff. Stateless, on the other hand, that's easy. It doesn't remember stuff. So, whatever you started with on day one, maybe a web server with some static content, if it runs for two weeks, at the end of those two weeks, it looks exactly the same as it did on day one, like nothing new has been updated or stored. So if that goes bang, we just bring it back up exactly how it was on the first day two weeks ago. So for us, that's stateful and stateless. Now then, just as a way to reinforce, maybe this quick restaurant analogy helps. A stateful restaurant would be one that remembers you. So you've been there before, and you walk up again, and the staff are like, oh, Mr. Poulten, we remember you. You like the table on the balcony with the city view. Let's see if we can get you up there again. Whereas a stateless restaurant, I don't know, that'd be more Mickey D's or something where they've got no idea that you've been before, and you take your tray, and you find your own table. Anyway, look, the general story these days is that Docker and Kubernetes are actually pretty darn good at both. I mean, they're the absolute business when it comes to stateless, but without any trace of stretching the truth, they are really good at stateful as well. So, let's go look a bit closer.

Low-hanging Fruit

Now, and I'm going to keep this as brief and as high level as I can because it can be a complex topic, but I do think we need some background and history real quick. Now, I don't think there's any doubt that there's a huge push towards modern cloud native and microservice designs and architectures. The premise is modern businesses need to be agile and a whole bunch of other buzzwords, but buzzwords aside, these are facts. Modern businesses needs to be more reactive and more adaptive than ever, and modern businesses are for the most part the sum of their applications, at least to the extent that crappy old sluggish apps equals crappy old sluggish businesses for the most part. Now, we might talk about it later, but anyone who remembers walking or driving to the video store to rent a movie on VHS knows that streaming from Netflix or whoever is way better. And obviously, most of those old VHS rental businesses are gone. But why? I mean, it's certainly not because we're not watching movies or TV anymore. On the contrary, actually. We're watching more than ever. So you might think those old movie and VHS rental companies would be kings and queens of the world, but they're not. I mean, they're gone. Why? Because they didn't react and adapt to change. Anyway, we need scalable adaptable businesses. The market's demanding it. Well, clouds are providing the infrastructure, and Docker and Kubernetes are providing the tools for building the apps. Now, you might remember from the module on containers we said that VMware and hypervisors revolutionized IT. The emphasis on IT there maybe rather than apps and businesses. Anyway, they dragged IT from the dark ages of wasted server resources, whereas now we're in the modern world where we're pushing resource utilization like we never pushed it before.

Hypervisor Virtualization

Let us keep our existing apps

- Simple migrations
- Made life easy

Let us keep our existing apps

- We've still got our legacy apps

Fabulous! Only, the VM thing is a bit of a two-edged sword. On the good side, it let us lift our existing applications from the physical world and drop them straight into the virtualized world, but on the bad side, it let us lift our existing applications from the physical world and drop them straight into the virtualized world. Wait, huh? Okay, stick with me. On the one hand, we can take our legacy apps, heritage apps, call them what you want, but we could take them without changing them and run them on virtual machines. Magic? Migrations literally couldn't have been easier, and now utilization was better. And you know what? Yeah, that's good, it's certainly better than not doing it, but it's not truly great. I mean, think about it. It did precious little to help make apps any better, and IT is supposed to be about the app, right? I mean, let's face it. All we were doing was taking our crappy old apps and just not having them be as wasteful, which I get it, I mean, it means there's less waste of business capital or whatever, but it hasn't helped us make our businesses more agile and flexible, at least not noticeably. Well, containers, and yes, we kind of can do the same sometimes, so lift our old crud and drop it straight into containers, but containers bring so much more to the table. So, like, when we come to containerize our apps, we really should be rethinking and refactoring them. Because like we said, business requirements have changed, and with clouds and containers, we've got everything we need now to build much better apps. And really, I am not talking about just better for IT or for me as a techie. I'm genuinely talking about better for the business and better for the customer, noticeably better.

Containers

We get to develop apps that are:
- modern
- scalable
- self-healing
- portable

We get to develop apps that are:
- modern
- scalable
- self-healing
- portable

But, this too is a two-edged sword. On the one hand, we're starting to develop and deliver new modern, scalable, self-healing, portable apps, but on the other hand, we are having to develop, and I'm sure you get it, modern, scalable, self-healing, portable apps. The point is yes, it's the way forward, and yes, we absolutely want to do business on those kinds of terms, but yeah, it takes pain and effort to get there. Only, check it out. On the effort front, there is low-hanging fruit, and that's your new or your greenfield apps, and it's anything stateless. I mean, Docker in

containers has done stateless since day one,
and Kubernetes as well, and it's a perfect fit.
And because it's so easy, it's usually where
people start, but it really is only the start.
There's a way bigger picture. So, let's switch
tack now and talk about stateful.

State & Legacy Apps

Okay, like we've said, Docker and
Kubernetes are absolutely magic when it
comes to stateless workloads, but when we
say that, it could be misconstrued to imply,
and it often has been, that they are not good
for stateful or traditional apps, which, let's
be fair, is still the staple of most enterprises.
Well, the good news is it is not true that
containers can't do stateful or even
traditional heritage apps. You know what? It
was just that these kinds of workloads are
harder, and I think this is the case with just
about anything that's new. The easy stuff
gets done first. But guess what? Containers
are not new anymore. This stuff is growing
up fast, and as Docker and Kubernetes have
matured, they've added the stuff that's
needed for stateful and traditional apps. I
mean, on the Docker technology front,
volumes and persistent storage, that's come

on leaps and bounds. And the same for Kubernetes. It's got a pretty comprehensive persistent storage subsystem. Now, while we're on with Kubernetes, it's also got a ton of other features and objects for stateful services. So, things like the Kubernetes Deployment object, that's great for stateless work, and don't stress if some of the terminology is new here. The point is Kubernetes has, and probably always has had, the stuff for stateless workloads. But on the stateful front, well, as well as things like persistent storage, there's stateful sets and other stuff, all of which are core to Kubernetes. Now we're high level here, so I'm sparing you the details, but the point is the primitives, and the objects, and everything else necessary, integrations into external storage systems, you name it, it's all there so you can do stateful work. So, Docker and Kubernetes definitely does stateful. Now, on the legacy, or heritage application front, if you're not ready to refactor your apps, but maybe you do want to move to a container platform, well, at least one example, of which there are others, but Docker, Inc. for an age now has had its modernizing traditional apps program where they make it super simple just to lift and shift some of your legacy apps into containers. Now, it's not an end goal in and of itself, but it is a step one in getting onto a modern container platform. So, look,

we're a big picture course, and I don't want
to bamboozle you with detail. The take-home
point is that Docker and Kubernetes, as
technologies have advanced massively, and
since, at the very least, 2018 and even earlier,
they've had the tools to deal with state and
the more difficult workloads. Brilliant.
Alright, let's recap.

Recap

Okay, so I feel like we've done a bit of
jumping around in this module, so I'll want
to give a coherent summary. At the end of
the day, technology is always about either
the business or the project, and modern
businesses and projects need to morph and
grow and deal easily with change. So it
stands to reason that our technologies need
to do the same. Like, if our tech can't adapt
and grow, then our businesses have got no
chance. No sweat though. We're living in a
golden age of technology where we've got all
the tools we need. I mean, cloud platforms
are providing us with things like
infrastructure on demand, while Docker and
Kubernetes give us the tools to build agile
scalable apps. So, Dynamic infrastructure
and tools to build dynamic apps, and I mean

entire apps. So we've talked a bit about modern cloud-native apps, you know, how we tend to build a useful app from lots of small parts that work together. Now early in the days of Docker, we really only had the tools to build the stateless parts of the app. For the persistent stuff, we'd still go to VMs. Well, these days, we can do the whole lot in containers. Docker and Kubernetes are both beyond the tipping point where it's feasible to run entire application stacks in containers, stateful and all. Now in saying that, I'm not saying that we have to do it that way. In fact, a lot of the time, we're actually going to be seeing application stacks that consist of containers, VMs, functions, and no doubt whatever else comes along, which is fine, and chances are Kubernetes is going to manage the whole stack. Also, as well as this modern cloud-native stuff, you can, if you so desire, lift and shift some of your legacy apps straight into containers. We said Docker, Inc. offers this modernizing traditional apps program, and they're not the only ones, but you can literally lift some of your older apps out of virtual machines and physicals into containers. So, there's choice, and with Docker and Kubernetes, you can pretty much do most things. I mean, yeah, there's a learning curve of course, and you need strategies to tackle it, but we've talked about that in the previous set of lessons. And you know what though, despite the effort required, for the sake of your career and your business, you should be starting to do this. I mean, if we go back to our video rental store analogy, and we're wrapping up on this point, but even Netflix, if I remember right, started out by posting DVDs to your letter box. My guess is they saw that the old video store on the high street, or strip mall, was dying out, so they started offering a postal service where you'd rent a movie and they would post it to you. But as an organization, they were open to admitting the flaws in their product, and they changed their business to streaming content, and I guess they've not looked back since. Now, look, of course I admit that Netflix isn't the perfect analogy for a lot of business, but their willingness to adapt and change probably is. I mean, I see banks and the likes that I used to work for rebranding and reengineering themselves pretty much as software companies, and they're willing to change the old models. And on the technology front, they're doing it with containers using Docker and Kubernetes. So yeah, containers. They're great for new modern apps, the stateless and stateful bits, and they're also an option for some of your older heritage apps, and they can totally sit alongside VMs and functions within the same app. And on that note, we're done on this topic. Coming up next, we're going to talk about whether this stuff is for the enterprise or just for startups.

Module 7 : Enterprise and Production Readiness

Enterprise and Production Readiness

Okay, a couple of questions that come up a lot: Are these technologies production ready, and are they for the enterprise? And they're good questions, so this is how we'll go about it. We'll cover Docker first because it was here first. Then we'll do Kubernetes. After that, we'll give the ecosystem a quick mention. Then we'll wrap up. But before just plowing in, and I don't want to patronize any of you here, but irrespective of what I say, obviously, deciding if something of production ready or ready for your business is your call, not mine because you know your business way better than I do. However, that said, I have spent a significant chunk of my career working in the financial sector, and for a big part of that, I was a storage guy at large retail banks. So believe me, I've personally been Mr. Risk Averse in some of the most risk-averse organizations out there. So, I'm not particularly quick to declare something production worthy. I mean, it's not like I've spent my entire life building web startups in the cloud. No. I know a thing or two about the enterprise. Anyway, even though I may feel that some things are production ready, the final decision is yours. Magic. Let's go talk about Docker.

Docker

Okay, so Docker. Is it production worthy, and is it fit for the enterprise? Well, we're going to find out. So, Docker the company and Docker the technology have been around for a while. The company started out as dotCloud around 2010, but then it rebranded itself as Docker, Inc. in, I think, 2013. Community Edition (CE)

- Free
- Quick release cycle
- Edge channel (fun/scary stuff)

Enterprise Edition (EE)

- Costs money
- Official support
- Patches
- Cautious release cycle
- Stability
- Extras
- Enterprise web UI
- Security features
- AD/LDAP
- Private registry
- Policies
- FIPS
- Pipelines...

Well, on the technology front, there's two main branches: Community Edition and Enterprise Edition. Now both of them can run on-prem and in the cloud, but I think the names say it all. Community Edition's aimed at, well, the community, so it's free to use, it's got a rapid release cycle, and it's got this edge channel if you want to live on the bleeding edge and play with all the exciting new stuff. Enterprise Edition though, well, it's kind of the same, but it's also different. I think, for starters, it's a pay-for product, and in exchange for your money, one of the things you get is support. So things like you can pick up the phone and get help from Docker when things go wrong, but you also get free patches and security fixes for 2 years. I think for Community Edition, it's something like half a year. Anyway, on the release and support front, compared to Community Edition, Enterprise Edition's got a slower release cycle. Pretty much everything that goes into it should be battle tested and stable. In fact, the Enterprise Edition doesn't even have an edge channel. It is all about stability. But each release gets 24 months of support, so things like phone support, as well as patches and security updates, which I think we just said compared to Community Edition is about 6 or 7 months. Aside from price and support though, you get a ton of extras. So, at its core, Community Edition and Enterprise Edition are the same. I'm talking about the code that starts and stops containers, that's the same, but bolted on around all of that, Enterprise Edition gets a ton more. There's things like a sophisticated web UI, and there's more security, for example. You can create users and groups that match your organizational structure. In fact, you can integrate with your corporate AD and just leverage users and groups from there. Also though, you get a private registry for storing your apps as Docker images. And like we said before, you can run this on-prem or in the cloud. So, either on your own private cloud or your own private area of a public cloud. The point is you can store your software in a secure, private repository that is owned and managed by you. Okay, and back to groups though. You can leverage groups to implement things like policies that support things like signing of images and maybe things like vulnerability scanning. What else? Oh yeah, you get a bunch of FIPS stuff, and you can even build workflows and pipelines. So, a bunch of value-add stuff that's really important to enterprises. And that's Docker. Is it production worthy or fit for your enterprise? Well, that's your call, but hopefully we've given you a bit of an idea. Now for Kubernetes.

Kubernetes

Okay, Kubernetes. Is this ready for production, and is it ready for the enterprise? Well, we know that Kubernetes came out of Google, it's open source like Docker, and it's got insane support from the community, like, all the big cloud players and all the big traditional enterprise tech companies, they're all over it, and that's not even mentioning the innovative startups. But, first things first.
On Premises

- Build your own

Cloud

- **Hosted (canned) options**

    - **AWS EKS**
    - **Azure AKS**
    - **Google GKE**

- **Build your own**

Like Docker, you can rock and roll with Kubernetes on-prem and in the cloud. And if you go for the cloud, there are a ton of canned options that I really like. So for example, AWS has its hosted Elastic Kubernetes Service, Azure's got AKS, the Azure Kubernetes Service, and Google's got GKE, Google Kubernetes Engine. Now, other clouds have got their own, but they're all essentially the same. The cloud provider hosts and manages the hard Kubernetes stuff, and we just deploy our apps to it. Okay, but if hosted isn't your thing, you can also build your own Kubernetes either on-prem or in the cloud. Now then, look, Kubernetes is a gigantic project, way bigger than Docker. I mean, the scope and breadth of what Kubernetes can do is awesome. Look, and I'm a Brit. I don't use that word very often. But honestly, the scope of what Kubernetes can do truly is awesome, and it's growing all the time, which, okay, is great. But no surprises, it's got its challenges, one of which is just keeping track of features. I mean, some features, they've been around for ages and they're rock solid, whereas others, you probably shouldn't even touch them if your life depends on it. Well, fortunately, to help us keep track of this, every Kubernetes feature goes through a set of well-defined stages.

Alpha
- Off by default
- Early code
- Uncertain future
- Not for production

Beta
- On by default
- Becoming stable
- Promising future
- Some details may change

GA
- Production ready*
- Solid future
- Stable
    - Code
    - Features

So the main ones here are alpha, beta or beta, and GA. Now, from a high level, alpha features have to be explicitly enabled, so they're turned off by default to stop you accidentally using them. What else? They're probably buggy, and you know what? They can get dropped without warning. So, generally steer clear. Certainly not for production. Features in beta though. I mean, these should be pretty stable, and they won't get dropped overnight, though some of the implementation detail might change. Oh, and they're enabled by default. Now, I've seen plenty of people use beta features in their production environments, in fact, a lot of us did this with deployments, but if you are doing that, just be careful. Anyway, GA is the gold standard, or the stamp of approval. Anything in GA is here for the long game, and it should be stable. And by that, I mean the code itself should be stable and good, but also, so should the way that the features are implemented and managed. That shouldn't really change. So, I think that's the story really. Alpha, that's scary; beta, that's for the brave and the early adopters; and GA, that's for the rest of us. Now then, yes Kubernetes is open source, but you know what? Google is still invested, and it has a ton of engineers on it. Cool. But do you know what? So does the likes of Microsoft and IBM and a ton of smallers as well. I think my point is the big boys are supporting Kubernetes, especially on their cloud offerings. And look, I know the public cloud isn't for everyone, but if you can, I definitely recommend you check out some of the hosted Kubernetes services. And if you're not wed to a particular cloud, personally, I like GKE on Google, but they're all pretty similar. For me, as much as I do love the fun of building stuff myself, I just wonder if from like a business-focused perspective, I don't know, I just wonder if we're better spending our time on other things. You know, like let Amazon, or Microsoft, or whoever build my Kubernetes. Sure, I mean, I'm going to hold the keys and manage it, I'm just not convinced I want to spend my company time building infrastructure anymore, especially when I can just go to my cloud provider and ask for something and get it. Look, I don't know, everybody's different, but maybe it's food for thought at least. Anyway, what else? Tons of companies from big to small are using Kubernetes every day in production, and I'm talking on-prem and in the cloud. And from the conversations I'm having, it is probably the hottest technology on most company's agendas right now. Good stuff. Well, time for a quick mention of the wider ecosystem before we recap.

Ecosystem

Okay, a quick word on the container ecosystem because Docker and Kubernetes, they are by no means the entire picture. If you go to any of the major events like DockerCon or KubeCon, you will see a ton of companies building up around them and filling in the gaps. You know, things like monitoring, and security, and machine learning. Tons of it. There's companies springing up offering just about everything you'd need to augment and enhance your Docker and Kubernetes environments. Now, I'm going to name any specific companies because, well, I guess it wouldn't be fair, but also, some of them just won't last, and that's an important point to consider. I mean, sure Docker and Kubernetes' technologies are going to be here for the long term, but some of the companies in the ecosystem certainly won't, and you're going to want to consider that when you're choosing who to use. But, that said, some of them are solid companies with great products, and you could do worse than checking them out and seeing where they can help. And that's it really. There's a really buoyant ecosystem, and they're offering some great stuff. Go check them out. Well, you know what, time for a quick recap.

Summary

Okay then, hopefully we've got a bit of an idea now when it comes to is this stuff ready for production, and is it for the enterprise? Because I think it goes without saying that yeah, it's definitely for cloud and startups. But we all know existing companies with existing products and customers, I don't know, those guys tend to have the bar set a bit higher. Anyway, we know that Docker's got a dedicated Enterprise Edition that's focused on stability and enterprise features. We mentioned steady release cycles with accompanying support. Plus, we also mentioned a bunch of features like private registries, a bunch of security stuff, pipelines, you name it, all geared at meeting enterprise needs. So, the call is yours, but that's the state of play with Docker. On the Kubernetes front, we said oh man, it is a huge platform, but every feature goes through alpha, beta, and GA, and there's an absolute ton of offerings in the community if you want an enterprise UI or whatever else. Again though, the call on whether it's production worthy or enterprise ready is yours, but I can tell you this, and it's the same with Docker, there's a ton of companies using it.

And in the Kubernetes space, the hosted cloud platforms are definitely worth checking out. Well, we finished things up by saying the ecosystem is absolutely thriving. And you know what? It's just a brilliant place if you're looking for the likes of monitoring, and logging, and a bunch of the other enterprisey stuff that's often not the core competency of a platform. And you know what? That's as done on this topic. Time for just one more though. Before we wrap up the course, let's have a quick chat about orchestration.

Module 8 : Orchestration

Orchestration

Now then, just in case orchestration is a brand-new concept to you, or maybe you've got a bit of an idea, but you're not 100% sure, well, this module's for you.

Team

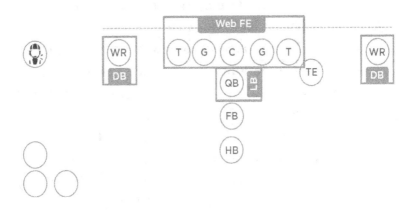

So, at a really high level, and I am running
the risk of embarrassing myself here seeing
as I'm no expert on American sports, but if
you take an American football team, there's
a bunch of players, and each one's got his or
her own job pretty much. Anyway, a bunch
of players and a bunch of different jobs, and
on their own individually, they're not really
that special. It's when they come together as
a team that the magic happens. But in order
to work as a team, they need organizing,
dare I say orchestrating? Boom, there we go.
That's our buzzword. And look, I know the
analogy's pretty cheesy, but stick with me. So
in sports like this, there's usually a coach
that's calling the plays. We'll put them here.
So, it's the coach's job to do all the
orchestrating, like telling people where to

77

stand and where to run or who to tackle, all that stuff. And you know what? Fans of American sports, give me a break here if I'm getting this wrong. At least I'm trying. Anyway, look, this coach, in a way, is orchestrating everyone so the overall team does something useful. Score a touchdown or prevent a down or something. Well, out there on the field, there's, well, let's say these big old guys that stand in the line at the front. You know the ones. They charge at each other, and then they, I don't know, it looks like they cuddle for a while. Well, comparing this to a cloud-native microservices application, these guys might be the application's web front end. Then the quarterback might be the load balancer, or the message broker, or the search API, whatever. And, I don't know, the wide receivers might be the database back end. Look, I don't know, and that's about all the positions that I know, so I'll stop there. But my attempted point is that the team is made up of individuals, and each one's got their own job. Some guys block, some run, some catch, some throw. All totally different things, but when organized and orchestrated, they achieve something with a purpose. Well guess what? The same goes for business applications. Funnily enough, they're also made up from a bunch of individual or small services, at least the modern cloud-native ones are. But when all of these different individual services are orchestrated, they come together as a useful app. Kind of like a sports team. Well, how was that for an analogy? Hopefully not bad for a Brit. Anyway, analogies, they're good and all, but let's take a bit of a closer look.

Orchestration

Okay, just about any modern app out there, certainly a production-worthy one, is going to be composed of multiple interlinked services that span multiple hosts, maybe even span multiple datacenters or clouds. And as soon as we start talking about lots of these apps, so each with lots of independent parts and requirements, we can easily be talking hundreds or thousands of containers with really complex architectures. And at scaling complexity like that, believe me, we do not want to be calling the shots manually.

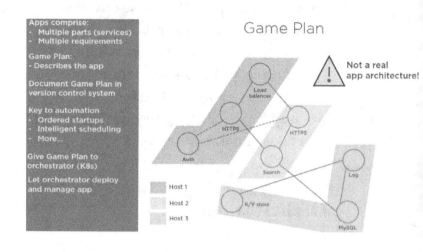

Game Plan

Not a real
app architecture!

Load
balancer

HTTPS

HTTPS

Auth

Search

Log

Host 1

Host 2

Host 3

K/V store

MySQL

So, for starters, we need a game plan,
something that describes how everything in
the app fits and works together. Things like,
well, first of all, just defining the different
services that make up the app, but as well,
where they should be deployed and at least
how they talk to each other. So networking,
message queues, APIs, all of that, it all needs
describing in the game plan. And please, I'm
sure you get this, but make sure that game
plan does not just exist inside your own head
or the head of one of your employees. It
needs to exist in a system, and we'll come to
that in a minute. Anyway, once the app or
the game plan is described, we need a way of
executing on it, and we normally use the
terms deploying and managing. And like we
just said, it cannot be manually, not when we
get to scale. Now, look, I know that this is
high level, but what we've talked about there

really is at the core of container orchestration. Define our app, how all the parts interact, provision the infrastructure, and then deploy and manage the app. That's orchestration. But it gives us great things. I mean, dependencies like ordered startup, scheduling services next to each other, or maybe some shouldn't be next to each other, so not starting on the same nodes as others or maybe not even in the same zone or whatever. All of this gets documented in the game plan. Then we give the game plan to an orchestrator, usually that's going to be Kubernetes, and we let the orchestrator deploy the app and manage it. So if usage ramps and we need more web servers or whatever, no sweat. Update the game plan, and the orchestrator makes it happen. It really is good stuff. Now, the main orchestrator out there is Kubernetes, and it is the absolute business. I mean, it's pretty much industry standard, and it does just about everything, but it is big, and the learning curve can be steep. But a smaller and simpler product is Docker Swarm. Now, at its core, it essentially does the same thing, deploy and manage microservices apps. It's just got a lot less features and a lot less momentum. And that's not me knocking it. I'm actually a big fan. It's really simple to use. It's just I think Kubernetes has the brighter future, and I think Docker, Inc. 's own adoption and support of Kubernetes is testament to that. Anyway, that's the big picture for orchestration. Let's do a super quick recap.

Summary

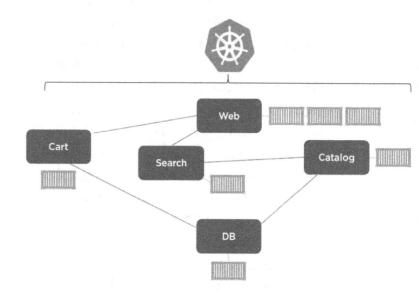

A quick refresher then. We talked about how modern apps are generally composed of multiple services. Think web service, search service, catalog, shopping cart, database, all that goodness. And they all work together, and we get a useful application. Well, generally speaking, each of these individual services runs in its own container, and if we need to scale one of the services, we just throw more containers at it, which is important actually. We don't make the container bigger to cope with demand, we just enlist more of the same container, and then the reverse if we need to scale down; we just take away some of the containers. Anyway, at scale, because this is a way oversimplified diagram, but things get complicated, really complicated. I mean, lots of services, many of which need to talk to each other, some need to live next to each other, some absolutely can't live next to each other, things need to scale up and down with business needs and the likes, and before you know it, you need a system just to manage everything. Well, that system is your orchestrator, and it's probably going to be Kubernetes. Okay, now, if all of this is new to you, I totally get that it can sound daunting and be hard to wrap your head around.

So we tried to compare it to an American football team where you've got a bunch of individuals with a bunch of different jobs and a coach with a game plan that makes sure everyone knows what their job is and kicks in the right direction. Well, in the cloud-native application world, the coach is your orchestrator, probably Kubernetes, the game plan is a description of your application, and the players are the different services in the app. And that's orchestration. But let me say this: If you are serious about your real-world apps, and I hope you are, well, you want to make orchestration a top priority. And that's it; however, join me in one more module for a really quick chat about some of the options that you have for taking your cloud native and container journey to the next level.

Module 9 : What Next?

What Next?

Alright then, here we are. Finished the course. And if I've done my job, you should be well up to speed on what Docker and Kubernetes are. I think, didn't we say at the beginning of the course that we'd give you enough so that you'd be able to hold your own talking about containers at the pub or at the coffee machine? Yeah, I'm pretty confident we've done that. But I know this, at least if you're anything like me, I forget stuff faster than I can learn it. So if you start getting rusty or think, you know what, I could read that book again, well obviously feel free to. But I get it that that takes time, and not many of us have time, so I purposefully placed a summary lesson at the end of most modules so that if you feel like you need a quick refresher, just watching the summaries might be enough. So where do you take your journey next? And this is an interesting one because we've pitched this course at pretty much everyone from developers and sysadmins all the way through to non-technical management. So where you go next is going to depend a lot on what your role is and where you see yourself going.

www.ingramcontent.com/pod-product-compliance
Lightning Source LLC
LaVergne TN
LVHW051537050326
832903LV00033B/4289